Mark for Starters

Mark
for
Starters

**A way to get into the life
and ideas of Jesus**

David Winter

Text copyright © 1995 David Winter

The author asserts the moral right to be
identified as the author of this work.

Published by
The Bible Reading Fellowship
Peter's Way, Sandy Lane West
Oxford OX4 5HG
ISBN 0 7459 2825 0
Albatross Books Pty Ltd
PO Box 320, Sutherland
NSW 2232, Australia
ISBN 0 7324 0914 4

First edition 1995
10 9 8 7 6 5 4 3 2 1 0

Acknowledgments
Unless otherwise stated, scripture is
taken from The Good News Bible
published by The Bible Societies/
HarperCollins Publishers Ltd, UK ©
American Bible Society 1966, 1971,
1976, 1992.

A catalogue record for this book is
available from the British Library

Printed and bound in Great Britain
by Cox and Wyman Ltd, Reading

CONTENTS

AUTHOR'S FOREWORD

You may never have read a single word of the Bible before, but you've decided to look into the world's best-selling book.

You may have listened to the Bible being read in church, or dipped into it over the years for yourself in a sporadic sort of way.

You may be a regular Bible reader, but you've never set out to get deeply into one of the Gospels.

Mark for Starters is for each of you, but in different ways. It takes the shortest of the four Gospels (the early accounts of the life and teaching of Jesus) and invites you to read it, assuming nothing beyond your willingness to give both Mark's Gospel and this book a few minutes of your time each day.

For the person totally new to the Bible, it invites you to get straight into the story of Jesus as Mark tells it, with all the help you may need to understand, appreciate and enjoy it.

For the sporadic reader, it offers an opportunity to tackle a book from the Bible in the same way as you would a novel, reading all of it over a relatively short period of time, with pointers, ideas and information to help you get the most from it.

And for the regular Bible reader, it invites you to immerse yourself for about forty days in Mark's Gospel and to gain a fresh insight into the 'core' of the Gospel material about Jesus.

Because this book is primarily for the person unfamiliar with the Bible, it assumes no prior knowledge at all of biblical ideas or background. Whenever a word occurs in Mark's Gospel that a modern reader might not recognize, or might misunderstand, there is a separate section at the end of the commentary with the kind of background and explanatory information you might find helpful.

Probably the best way to use this book is to start each session by reading through the relevant part of Mark's Gospel (preferably in the Good News version). Then read the material given in *Mark for Starters* and any separate section that relates to ideas in that passage. Finally, having done that, go back and read the Bible section again.

We speak in English of 'gospel truth'. The implication is that the Gospels deal in truth in some special and even unique way.

As you get into Mark's Gospel, I think you will find that 'gospel truth' is, indeed, special and unique, because it is the truth of God shown to us in the life of his Son, Jesus. In the case of Mark's Gospel, that 'truth' is related by someone who was close to the original events and offers to the reader a unique and authentic picture of the 'man from Nazareth'.

ABOUT MARK AND HIS GOSPEL

Somewhere between the years 4BC and AD30 lived a man whose life changed the world. He was unknown during his lifetime outside his own, small country. He wrote no book, and when he died he left behind a pathetically small band of followers—about 120 in all. But in any history of the human race this man has a place of honour. And today, 2,000 years later, the movement begun by those first followers is by a long way the largest religion in the world, and literally billions of people revere him as the 'Son of God'. That man is, of course, Jesus.

What you are going to read is the earliest account of his life, written about thirty-five years after his death, probably by one of his first followers, John Mark.

He probably wrote his book because soon there would have been very few eyewitnesses of Jesus still alive, and it was obviously necessary for the young Christian Church to have a reliable account of the life and teaching of its founder.

If the book was indeed the work of Mark—and most experts think that it was—then he had access to the apostles, the first leaders of the Church, who had been personally appointed by Jesus. Mark is mentioned in the book of the Acts of the Apostles several times. We read of him as a young man at his mother's home, where the Jerusalem church met in the early days, and later as a companion and helper of St Paul. And some people think he is the young man mentioned in the Gospel (Mark 14:51–52) who fled naked from the scene of Jesus' arrest.

It's probable that Mark also had access to a collection of sayings and stories of Jesus which was in circulation in the early years of the Church but has long been lost. Possibly it was never committed to writing, but was passed on orally, by Christians who learnt the sayings and stories by heart.

Mark's is almost certainly the oldest of the Gospels—it looks as though Matthew and Luke were familiar with Mark's book and used it as a source for their own Gospels. Mark probably wrote his book in the sixties AD.

Strangely, as we shall see, we probably don't have the whole book that he originally wrote. For some inexplicable reason the very last part seems to be missing—or was never completed. Yet in more fundamental ways Mark's story is complete. It sets out to show how a vital battle between good and evil was fought out in the brief three years of the public ministry of Jesus—and he's in no doubt who was the winner in the end!

Mark 1:1–13

Now for the Good News!

This first section begins by telling us that the book we are going to read is 'Good News' (with capital letters!). That simply signals that it's a 'Gospel' (the word just means 'good news'). It's good news about a person, Jesus Christ. And it's good news that starts way back in history, with the prophet Isaiah, 600 years before Jesus. He told people that one day a 'voice' would call in the wilderness telling the Jewish people to get ready for the coming of good news. For Mark, John the Baptist's was that voice and Jesus was the good news.

John the Baptist was a rather strange, awesome preacher. He came on the scene in about AD27, in the wilderness of Judea, quite near Jerusalem. He told the Jews that they must get ready for the coming of someone greater than he was—and that the way to get ready was to turn away from their sins and be baptized. This was a ritual washing, in which they were dipped in the River Jordan, or had its water poured over them, to show they wanted to make a completely new start. Then—and only then— would they be ready for this marvellous person God was sending to them. He wouldn't baptize them with water, but with 'the Holy Spirit'. That probably means that they would be clean on the 'inside', as it were, as well as on the 'outside'. The water would wash their bodies; the Holy Spirit would 'wash' their hearts.

The 'Holy Spirit' is not an easy idea to get hold of. Perhaps the simplest way is to think of him as 'God-inaction'—God being involved in everything that goes on in the world he has made. Mark says that when Jesus came to be baptized by John, the Holy Spirit 'came down on him like a dove'. If you can imagine a bird landing gently on someone's head, you've got the picture! God's Holy Spirit settled on Jesus—marked him out, if you like, as God's 'own dear Son'. This man was somebody very special.

But the next thing the Holy Spirit did was to make Jesus go into the desert, where for forty days he was put to the test by Satan—God's 'opponent'. The task Jesus had been given to do was very, very demanding, and before he set out on it he was given a 'taster' of how difficult it would be. The desert of Judea is a barren, hot, rocky wilderness— forty minutes there would be enough for most of us, let alone forty days! But to the physical discomfort was added the inward 'testing' by Satan, who personifies all that is in opposition to the will of God. Jesus survived both tests— with a little help from some heavenly friends ('angels came and helped him').

Satan

'Satan' is the name the Bible gives to God's enemy—the devil, in ordinary language. 'Satan' simply means 'adversary', and it's probably simplest to think of him as the personification of everything that opposes God and goodness. Satan's power is effective in lives that are open to him, but is strictly limited.

For Mark, the life of Jesus can be seen as a running battle between the powers of darkness (represented by Satan and his demonic helpers) and the power of God 'earthed' in his Son.

Nothing in what the Bible actually says about Satan justifies the legendary picture of a figure with horns and a forked tail! Instead, he is seen as a sort of 'non-person', a malign negative force trying to frustrate the will of God.

Modern people have problems relating to the idea of a personal 'tempter'. But most of us are familiar with an evil and negative 'force' in our lives and in the world. We know what it is to be 'tempted', and sometimes behind it we sense the ill-will of our 'tempter'.

2

Mark 1:14–20
A sudden change of jobs

The section begins with a summary of the message that Jesus brought—the 'Good News from God'. The 'time' had come (the 'time' predicted by Isaiah, the moment when God would intervene); the 'kingdom of God' was near; people needed to turn away from their sins (as John the Baptist had called them to do) and accept the message.

We shall come across the phrase 'the kingdom of God' many, many times in Mark's Gospel. Very often the stories Jesus told were to illustrate the idea of the 'kingdom'. In fact, if you were asked to summarize the message of Jesus in four words, they would have to be 'the kingdom of God'.

What he meant by it was the rule of God—the 'kingdom' was where the king 'ruled'. He was telling people that it was now, at this moment, possible for people to put themselves under the 'rule' of their just and loving Father God, and begin to live in his 'kingdom'. In that kingdom, values would be different, ambitions would be transformed, life would be lived as God intended. That was his 'good news'—and the way into the kingdom was by turning away from sin and accepting the message. That was what Jesus preached as he came back from the desert into his home district of Galilee—the area around the famous lake.

Lake Galilee is a very beautiful sight, with its blue waters and surrounded by hills. But to many of the local men it was their place of work—fishing was an important business. And the first people Jesus called to follow him and be his 'disciples' were fishermen: Simon, Andrew, James and John.

We know from John's Gospel that they already knew Jesus. They had been followers of John the Baptist, and he had told them that the time had come for them to leave him and follow Jesus. So probably the rather abrupt invitation which Mark records—'Follow me!'—was not quite as sudden or unexpected as he makes it sound.

Jesus added what we might call an extra inducement. If they followed him, he would teach them to 'catch men' (actually, in the original language, 'people'). This sounds a bit ominous, rather like those unpleasant cults who 'fish' people in and then brainwash them.

In fact, I think he simply meant that he would raise their sights from the rather limited business of catching fish to the much more satisfying prospect of sharing the 'good news' with people. We could put it like this, 'Follow me, and I'll put you in the people business!' Or even, 'Follow me, and I'll give you a whole new set of goals for life'. That's quite a promise.

Apparently it was enough for the four erstwhile fishermen, anyway. They downed their nets, abandoned the ships (we can feel a bit sorry for poor Zebedee, 'left... with the hired men') and set off with Jesus on an adventure that would take them to some situations they could never have dreamt of.

Disciple

The word simply means 'learner'. A disciple was someone who was committed to following a particular teacher's philosophy or religion. The disciples of Jesus—and earlier of John the Baptist—voluntarily agreed to follow them, and shape their lives and beliefs by their teaching.

3

Mark 1 : 2 1 – 3 4
The battle with evil gets under way

All the events in this section took place on one day—a Saturday, the Jewish 'sabbath'. For Jews, all work of any kind is prohibited on this day, and eventually Jesus would run into conflict with the religious leaders over his insistence that healing the sick was not 'work'.

This day seems to have begun and ended with the driving out of 'demons' or 'evil spirits'. Jesus was a person who spoke with 'authority'—he didn't just repeat or enlarge on what others were saying, like the Jewish teachers, but took it upon himself to tell people God's message 'straight'. The crowd noticed the difference: this man had his own 'authority'—he didn't get it second hand.

But he also took authority over evil. That's the meaning behind these stories—rather strange ones, to us—about the driving out of demons. During his ministry, many people presented themselves to Jesus who were, we would probably say, seriously mentally disturbed. But there was a particularly evil element in these cases. Jesus saw their situation not just as a medical problem, but as a spiritual one. In some strange way, evil had got a hold on them, so that they were split personalities—driven by an evil force that was like a separate personality within them.

And he assumed authority to drive out this evil. The evil spirits, Mark says, recognized that authority (see verses 24 and 34) and obeyed it. So whatever else these stories mean to us today, they certainly tell us that Jesus Christ has ultimate power over evil—and that, too, has got to be good news.

Between the exorcisms we have a few more 'normal' healings of people, including Simon's mother-in-law and then, after nightfall, when the sabbath was officially over, crowds of people who gathered outside the house where Jesus was staying.

It must have been an amazing sight—the little seaside village of Capernaum crowded with ill and handicapped people, many being carried, and the whole scene, presumably, lit by hand-held torches. Jesus healed 'many', Mark says—not 'all' (verse 33), because his healing was always personal and individual.

As the first day of the rest of his life, as it were, this Saturday had been something rather special!

Exorcism

In the time of Jesus the practice of 'casting out' evil spirits or demons, which we usually call 'exorcism', was quite common. It was believed that God's enemy, Satan, could invade the body of a person who let him in, and could only be evicted by prayer in the name of God. It's notable, however, that Jesus exorcised in his own name.

Exorcisms still occur, though less commonly, when it is felt that a person's mental condition is the result of some evil power or experience that has rooted itself in them. The exorcist, usually a Christian minister, calls on the evil to leave the person 'in the name of Jesus Christ'.

Mark places his accounts of exorcisms by Jesus at the start of his story to illustrate what he means when he says that Jesus acted 'with authority'. He sees the whole ministry of Jesus (the three years or so from his baptism to the crucifixion) as one long contest between the power of good and the power of evil. But right at the start we are given a clue as to the outcome. Jesus has been given authority over all the forces of evil, and in the end that will be recognized by everyone.

4

Mark 1 : 3 5 – 4 5
Jesus, preacher and teacher

As we've seen, Jesus had had a very busy Saturday. Most of us would have reckoned we'd earned a lie-in on Sunday morning! But here he is, long before dawn, slipping out of the house and going to a 'lonely place' to pray. Perhaps he sat on the shore of the lake, or on the hillside overlooking it. It's very interesting that even the Son of God needed to pray—he needed his Father's strength and help each day.

It's also interesting that the disciples couldn't really understand this. When they found he wasn't in the house, they went out looking for him, apparently because another crowd had turned up for healing. Jesus refused to go back to Capernaum, explaining that his task was to carry the message to all the other towns and villages too.

And that was what he did, summarized here as 'preaching in the synagogues and driving out demons'.

All through his ministry Jesus took every opportunity he had to preach and teach in the synagogues. In fact, it was the first thing he had done in Capernaum. He was not interested in being known just as a miracle-worker or exorcist—he also always explained what he was doing and what it meant. He wanted the people to understand who he was, why he had come, and how they could enter into the kingdom of God.

In the next miracle, the healing of a man with a 'dreaded skin disease', we come across an idea which runs all through Mark's story. After healing the man, Jesus sternly warns him not to tell anyone about it. As we shall see, many of the people Jesus healed (and the spirits he 'cast out') were given this warning, almost as though he didn't want anyone to know that he was the 'One sent by God'. There's been a lot of discussion over the years as to why this warning was given and what Mark wants us to understand by it.

Some people think it was practical: Jesus would have been utterly swamped by crowds if every sick person in the land had come to him. Some think it was as a test of faith. Jesus wanted people to believe he was the Messiah without the help of miracles. And some believe it was because Jesus was working to a plan, and he hadn't yet reached the point in the plan where he was ready to 'go public'. At this point, only the disciples (and they very gradually) were to have their eyes opened to the truths of the kingdom of God. Or, of course, it may have been for all three reasons!

This 'dreaded skin disease' is usually called 'leprosy', but in fact it was definitely not the disease which is known as 'leprosy' nowadays. It was obviously highly contagious and incurable, and the unfortunate people who contracted it were forbidden to live in their homes or villages. So to be a 'leper' was really to be a social outcast, as well as to have an incurable, disfiguring and disabling disease. No wonder this man 'begged for help'—and no wonder Jesus was 'filled with pity' for him.

Synagogues

Jewish worship in the time of Jesus had two focal points—the temple in Jerusalem, and the local synagogues, which were to be found in every village and town, and far beyond Judea and Galilee, too. Originally it was intended that the worship of God should be centred on the temple, which we shall think about later. But political and other developments meant that many Jews couldn't get to the temple regularly, so the local 'synagogue' (or 'meeting place') became the normal centre of sabbath services. The synagogue service was built around the reading and explanation of the Law (the 'Torah'), based on the Law of Moses in the Old Testament, but greatly expanded and extended. There were also prayers and psalms.

Mark 2:1–12
Doubly cured

For this story we move back to Capernaum, on the shores of the lake, where Jesus had done his first miracles. Perhaps because of that, an enormous crowd had gathered, presumably outside Peter's house. Anyway, it was so large that four men carrying their paralysed friend couldn't even get near the door. So, showing great initiative, they climbed up on to the flat roof, lifted off some of the wooden slats and the thatch covering, and lowered their friend down on his mat, right in front of Jesus.

Jesus was impressed by their faith and gave the man on the mat what he most needed—which wasn't, to the surprise of the bystanders (and probably of the four friends, too!), healing from his paralysis, but the forgiveness of his sins.

That also started some muttering among the teachers of the Law, who taught that God was the only one who could forgive sins. Jesus knew what they were going on about, and decided to settle the issue with a demonstration rather than an argument. As it was impossible for a mere human being to heal a paralysed man or to forgive sins—both were equally impossible—he would show them that 'the Son of Man' had authority to do both. They couldn't see whether his sins were forgiven, but they could see him stand up, pick up his mat and walk off! Again, no wonder the crowds said to each other, 'We have never seen anything like this.' After all, God had never been present in a human being before in the way he was in Jesus.

There's one other very interesting point in this story. We tend to put physical health above everything else. People say, 'So long as you've got your health...' But this story reminds us that sin—that destructive principle that cuts us off from God in the same way as leprosy cut people off from their community—is actually more serious even than sickness.

Forgiveness may also be the way to real health for us. And the absence of it may be 'paralysing' our lives.

Mark 2 : 1 3 – 2 8
The new versus the old

There are three stories here, and each of them tells of a clash between the 'new' approach to religion, as represented by Jesus, and the 'old', as represented by the beliefs and customs of that time.

The first story is of Jesus calling the 'tax collector' Levi to follow him and be his disciple. This upset the 'teachers of the Law'—the religious leaders—who were even more annoyed when Jesus joined Levi, some of his tax-collecting friends and other 'outcasts' for a meal. The 'outcasts' were probably prostitutes and other morally undesirable people, who were banned from the synagogue and shunned by respectable folk.

Jesus' answer is short and to the point. He hasn't come for respectable people, but outcasts. As he puts it, 'If you're well you don't need the doctor.'

The next story contrasts the approach of Jesus to fasting with that of John the Baptist. Fasting—denying yourself food, as an act of religious discipline—was common among the Jews, and taken to be a sign of serious devotion to God. So why didn't Jesus and his disciples fast?

The answer of Jesus was not that fasting was 'wrong', but that it was inappropriate while he was around! His presence in the world created joy and generosity, not hardship and pain. He came to heal the sick and feed the hungry, as we've already seen. So, there would be plenty of time to fast one day... but not yet!

It was much the same with the sabbath. The Pharisees

objected to the disciples of Jesus picking ears of corn as they walked through a field—this was 'work', and all work was forbidden on the sabbath. The answer of Jesus was to remind them that the great King David, whom they all respected, had sat lightly to the rules when he thought it was right. Jesus went beyond that, though: 'The Son of Man'—the way he often referred to himself—is 'Lord even of the Sabbath'. The day of rest was created by God for the benefit of people, not to be a burden round their necks. As the 'Lord of the Sabbath' he claimed the right to set them free to enjoy it.

Verses 21 and 22 sum up this little section. Jesus had come with a radically new approach to religion, not based on rules and traditions, but on love and joy. That was why he wanted to eat meals with outcasts! The new and the old sit uncomfortably together, like new wine in old wineskins—they were made of leather, and old ones were dry and shrivelled up, and couldn't take the bubbly new wine without bursting.

So the 'new wine' of the teaching of Jesus needed new wineskins. If the old religious approach tried to contain it, it would simply burst apart. Which is exactly what happened!

Tax collectors

The tax collectors, or 'publicans', as the old translations called them, were Jewish people who collected taxes for the hated Roman occupiers. They were regarded as traitors by their own people, and also as cheats, because it was widely believed that they took more money in taxes than was strictly required, and pocketed the difference.

Sabbath

The 'sabbath' was Saturday—the seventh day of the creation story in the beginning of the book of Genesis. On that day, God 'rested' from his work (Genesis 2:2). The Jewish religious Law commanded that human beings, made in God's likeness, should also rest on the seventh day of every week—hence the 'sabbath' (the word means 'rest'). So the Fourth Commandment says that 'Six days you shall labour and do all your work, but the seventh day is a Sabbath to the Lord your God. On it you shall not do any work...'

By the time of Jesus this simple command had been complicated by a massive list of petty rules and regulations, so that something intended to be a blessing to people had become a tedious burden for many—and for some it became a stick with which to beat others!

Mark 3:1–19

The crowds—and the Twelve

One more miracle performed on the sabbath drives home the point that Jesus saw the sabbath as an opportunity to 'help' and not to 'harm' people. So he healed the man with a paralysed hand—and by doing it incensed the Pharisees to such an extent that they went to meet their avowed enemies, the party of Herod (who sided with the Romans), in order to begin to plot the death of Jesus.

Meanwhile Jesus had moved away from the towns to the lakeside, where a large crowd gathered, drawn from near and far. Jesus addressed the crowd from a boat, but presumably left it in order to heal many sick people. Once again he was confronted by people with 'evil spirits', who recognized him as the Son of God, but were subject to his authority—a great theme of Mark's Gospel.

When he finally drew away from the crowds it was in order to choose his central core of disciples, whom he called 'apostles' (the word simply means 'messengers'). Mark lists the twelve names, including some who subsequently became very well known, like Simon Peter, James, John, Andrew and Thomas; one who became notorious, Judas Iscariot; and several who are virtually never heard of again, though they presumably witnessed the resurrection and became messengers of Jesus in the early Church. His choice is a reminder that all Jesus requires of those he calls is that they faithfully do what he has chosen them to do. Of course, it's also a reminder that even among those who claim to be the closest followers of Jesus there may be traitors to the cause!

Mark 3:20–34
The opposition

We haven't heard anything so far about the family of Jesus. We know from the other Gospels that his mother was Mary, who was married to a carpenter called Joseph, and that he had at least two brothers. By now, it's possible that Joseph was dead. 'Family', at that time, meant much more than the 'two parents and two point six children' of modern Western custom! It included everyone who was related to you—cousins, aunts, uncles, second cousins... the lot! You could think of it as your 'clan' or 'tribe'.

Well, the 'clan' turned up to try to restrain Jesus. Perhaps they'd caught wind of the plot to kill him. At any rate, they decided this was all too much—a famous rabbi in the family was one thing, but an 'extremist' who went about upsetting the authorities and causing scandal was another! So they 'set out to take charge of him'.

At the same time, the religious leaders who had come from Jerusalem to check on this new preacher and miracle-worker arrived on the scene. They had a novel explanation for Jesus' ability to cast out evil spirits: 'He does it by invoking the chief of demons, Beelzebul.' That way they could damage Jesus twice over—by explaining away his successful exorcisms, and by implying that he was in league with the forces of evil.

Jesus countered it with cold logic. 'How can Satan drive out Satan?' The only one who can take charge of a situation is the one who has the superior power (that's the point of his remark about the 'strong man'). If he has cast out evil spirits, it is simply because he has greater power than they do.

He then added a warning to these 'experts' in religious Law. To allege that what was actually the work of the Spirit of God was the work of the devil was to commit the only unforgivable sin—what Jesus calls 'an eternal sin'. All other sins can be forgiven, and all evil words, too—but not the sin of ascribing to evil what is in fact the work of God.

Now Mark brings the family back into the picture. The crowd expected Jesus to take notice of what his mother and brothers had come to say. In fact, without implying any disrespect to his family (and the words in the original are quite 'neutral'), Jesus makes it clear that doing what God requires is the test for members of his 'family', rather than ties of blood. So the people in the crowd who believed in him and followed him were his 'mother and brothers'.

Mark 4:1–20
The answer's in the soil

We've seen already how Jesus 'taught' by arguing and disputing with his opponents. Now Mark introduces us to another way of 'teaching'—by telling 'parables', stories with a 'hidden' meaning... rather like Aesop's fables.

This one is very well known: the parable of the sower. Using something all his hearers would have been familiar with—a farmer scattering seed on his land—Jesus makes a simple but telling point. The difference in the crop does not depend on the seed (all of which is good), but on the quality of the soil. No matter how good the seed, if it lands on rocky ground, or among thorns, or on the path, it can't be expected to grow. But if it lands on good soil, then it multiplies—perhaps as much as a hundred times.

Apparently the disciples had some difficulty getting the message! In the first place, they seemed to find it strange that Jesus taught in parables, instead of plainly. But he explained that he used parables because they sorted out the true seekers (who would receive the 'secret of the kingdom') from those who 'look but don't see and listen but don't understand'. This is another theme of Mark's Gospel: that there is a 'secret' about Jesus, and people need to be initiated into it. Only at the right time would the 'secret' become public knowledge. Parables helped to preserve the secret, while making the truth crystal clear to those who possessed the key to it.

When he had told them this, quoting some rather harsh words of the prophet Isaiah about the people of his own day, Jesus went on to unpack the parable for his disciples. The 'seed' is 'God's message'—that's the heart of it. It's a good message, which brings a marvellous harvest when sown in good soil. But some only retain the message for a short while, giving it up when the going gets tough. Some allow the worries and concerns of life to distract them from it. Some lose the message almost the moment they hear it, snatched away by the Enemy.

But there are also those who are the 'good soil', and in them the message takes root and grows, and brings a bumper harvest.

Parables

Parables are stories with a meaning—we used to be told 'earthly stories with a heavenly meaning', and that gets very close to it. They were common in the time of Jesus (and we still use them today). He used them to get across often hard truths, and also to explain or illustrate what the kingdom of heaven (or of God) is 'like'—'The kingdom of God is like this...' is a typical introduction to a parable. In trying to understand their meaning we need to use our imaginations, of course, but also sometimes it's necessary to know the 'context'—often Jesus told parables to illustrate the situation which the Jewish people would be in if they were to reject him as their Messiah. In other words, some parables apply to all people at all times, but some are specific to that particular time in history. It's often important to spot the difference!

Mark 4:21–34
Three short parables

You don't light a lamp and then hide it under the bed. With that strikingly obvious comment Jesus warned his hearers that nothing in the end will be hidden; all will be revealed. He was probably referring to his parables, which, as we've seen, some people found difficult to understand. 'Pay attention to what you hear—you're being given something important and valuable. Be sure you make the most of it!' The person who understands a bit will understand more and more, but the person who completely fails to accept the message will lose even the little grasp of the things of God which he now has. It sounds very harsh, but of course in fact it simply explains what happens when any of us faces a new idea—some close their minds to it completely, and so miss out on what it may offer them. He's asking his hearers to be open-minded about his radical new message—'Listen, if you have ears!'

The next parable is another farming one. The kingdom of God is like a farmer, who sows his seed and then waits while it grows. He doesn't know how it happens, but eventually the seed grows into plants and the plants produce grain. When the corn is ripe, harvest time has arrived. We don't have to know how God will bring in his kingdom, we just have to have faith and patience to believe that he will.

Much the same point is made in the third of these brief parables. The kingdom of God is like a mustard seed, which is very tiny, but produces eventually a large bush with branches where the birds can make their nests. From very small things God can bring very great ones, if only we trust him.

Mark 4 : 35 – 41
Jesus calms the storm

There's no doubt this miracle poses problems for the modern reader! We understand about meteorological matters—highs and lows and depressions and so on—and we know that the weather is shaped by many complicated factors, often far away across seas or even continents. So we tend to be a bit sceptical about a man—even the Son of God—who can tell a storm to stop... and it does!

This story is in three of the Gospels, which means that it was part of the 'core' of teaching about Jesus that was treasured and passed on by the first Christians. So clearly it has its roots in a real event. What I mean is, something obviously happened that the disciples remembered and felt was very significant, so that it was passed on to the early generations of Christians.

And what happened must have been more or less what we read in this story. The disciples—experienced fishermen, several of them—were on Lake Galilee when a sudden storm blew up. These storms, or squalls, are typical of this lake and still happen today. They come up virtually without warning, and end very suddenly, but while they last they are very violent. When this storm broke, it was so severe that even the disciples were afraid that the boat was about to sink. Meanwhile (and I suspect this is the heart of the story), Jesus was asleep in the stern of the boat 'with his head on a pillow'. Not much panic there!

They woke him with words of complaint: 'Don't you care that we're about to die?' His answer was to counter that rather cruel accusation. Of course he cared, and they weren't going to die—look, the storm is to be quietened, the waves are to be still. Didn't they trust him? 'Have you still no faith?' The whole incident was about their trust in Jesus, rather than his power over the elements.

But (notice the word—in contrast to his challenge to their faith) 'they were terribly afraid': not now of the storm, which was past, but of a man who could demand obedience even of the wind and waves. It seems a healthier fear than their earlier one!

How this event occurred is not for me, or anyone, to say. The simplest explanation is that the words of Jesus coincided with the sudden blowing out of the storm. But I suppose there is nothing incongruous in the idea of the Son of God taking charge of the elements of his Father's creation in an awesome demonstration of power. Neither seems to me to be the point of the story, which is clearly about faith (read it again, if you don't believe me). If we have faith in Jesus, there is nothing to fear. That's what the disciples had to learn.

Mark 5:1-20

Jesus and a mob of demons

This is one of the strangest stories in the Gospels. A poor, demented man lived among the tombs in a burial place near the lake. He was obviously quite a well-known character locally. People had tried restraining him with chains and even irons, but such was his strength that he always broke free from them. So it seems they had left him to it, and he wandered through the hills and the burial area, 'screaming and cutting himself with stones'. Those who work with seriously disturbed people will recognize the symptoms.

As soon as this man met Jesus, he fell on his face and screamed out words of recognition—as in other stories of demonic possession in the Gospels, he knew who Jesus was, and feared that he would take control over his condition. Jesus asked him his name, and he answered 'Mob' ('Legion'—'Regiment'—in other translations)... because he felt himself to be not one but many people. I suppose he suffered from a kind of multiple schizophrenia.

He recognized Jesus, but Jesus also recognized him: he saw that at the root of this man's desperate condition lay some kind of bondage to evil, and it was that power of evil in the world that Jesus had come to confront. We've already seen the early skirmishes in this battle. Now comes a major one!

The power of evil which Jesus recognized was not just an abstract 'principle', but a malign and wicked force—perhaps we should give it a capital 'F' and call it 'Force'—opposing all that he stood for. So it, or he, could be called the Adversary,

'Satan', and it or he could take many forms, including multiple demons, which afflicted the poor man in this case.

What followed was a very dramatic exorcism, in which the demons left the man and entered into a nearby herd of 2,000 pigs, sending them rushing over a cliff into the lake to be drowned. This caused such terror in the neighbourhood that the local people asked Jesus to move on.

But the man was healed! Instead of screaming and hurting himself, they found him 'sitting there, clothed and in his right mind'. Indeed, he wanted to become a follower of Jesus and stay with him, but instead (in total contrast to most of the people Jesus healed) he was told to go back to his family and tell them what the Lord had done for him. You can imagine their utter astonishment when he did!

Modern readers will find the whole story rather difficult—the idea of demon possession seems to have more to do with horror movies than real life. And I've even heard people complain that it was cruel to send the demons into the pigs to terrify and then destroy them.

But we have to see it through the eyes of first-century Palestine, not twentieth-century Western culture. Evil is real: we all know that. And evil takes many forms. God sent Jesus into the world to confront, oppose and destroy the forces of evil wherever they were to be found—and in this case they were found in the life of a distressed man, made (like all of us) in the image of God, but turned into a wild, tormented being by their presence.

If you read the story carefully, you will find that while Jesus released the man from the evil spirits (verse 13) he said nothing about them going into the pigs. That was the conclusion of 'the men who had been taking care of the pigs', and it was exactly the sort of interpretation which a person of their time would have put on it. Possibly the man's screams terrified the pigs, and they fled in a panic over the edge of the cliff. But there's no doubt that the man who had been possessed would have been reassured to see that what had left him had not only gone somewhere else, but been destroyed in the process.

Incidentally—though it has nothing to do with the deep significance of the story—pigs were, of course, 'unclean' for the Jews, and consequently we can assume these animals were being raised for the benefit of the Roman occupiers. In other words, there wouldn't have been much sympathy from the local Jewish people either for the pigs, or the pig-keepers!

Mark 5:21–43
Two sick women

This is a story about two women, one a girl of twelve, the other an adult. Their lives were not connected, except through the events which are related here—and then only by accident, as it were.

The little girl was desperately ill, and her father, Jairus, who was a synagogue official, turned to Jesus for help. That in itself is fairly remarkable, because the respectable religious people seemed very wary of Jesus. Still, it was an emergency, and he was desperate. So he threw himself down in front of Jesus and begged for his help—in words that expressed real faith that Jesus could heal her. So Jesus started off towards their house.

As he was pushing his way through the crowd, the second woman came into the story. She too was desperate, though not dying. She had suffered from menorrhagia—excessive bleeding during menstruation—for twelve years. Despite spending all her money on doctors and cures, she had actually got worse. On top of the discomfort and weakness it caused, such a condition also excluded her from worship in the temple, normal social contacts and from her husband's bed. You can read the very strict rules in Leviticus 15:25–27. So she was not only ill with a very distressing condition, but a social outcast—and had been for twelve years.

Like Jairus, she believed that Jesus could heal her—'if I just touch his clothes'. I imagine she must have realized that if she did touch him, he would also be made unclean, according to the Jewish Law. But that didn't stop her. She touched his cloak.

And at that moment the bleeding stopped. She knew she was healed.

However, Jesus 'knew the power had gone out of him'—a fascinating insight into his healing ministry. 'Who touched my clothes?' he asked, and eventually the woman, very scared to be found out, knelt in front of him and admitted it was her. Jesus didn't seem very put out, and assured her that it was her faith that had made her well—she was to 'go in peace'.

Two things are worth noticing. First, he called her 'my daughter', words of warmth and acceptance he is never recorded having used to anyone else. Her family might have cut her off, but she was welcome in his!

Secondly, he simply went on his way towards the house of Jairus. If you refer back to Leviticus (15:27), anyone touching a person with such a discharge was to wash his clothes and bathe with water and be unclean until nightfall. Jesus just ignored the rules, and by doing so declared all these sexual taboos to be part of the 'old order' which he had come to change.

While all this was happening, however, there was bad news for Jairus. The message came that his daughter was now dead. But Jesus paid no attention—'Don't be afraid, only believe'... only! He added, rather mysteriously, that the child wasn't dead, but 'sleeping'. Whether he meant that she was in a coma, or deeply unconscious, or meant the 'sleep' of death, we can't guess. But in any case, as we read, he healed her, even asking her family to give her something to eat!

Mark 6:1–29
The death of John the Baptist

Jesus went back to his home town, Nazareth, to find that 'local boy makes good' isn't always true! 'Familiarity breeds contempt' seems more appropriate here—after all, this young man had been the local carpenter, so how can he be working miracles? The result of all this scepticism was that he couldn't do any miracles there—apart from 'a few sick people' who were healed.

His next task was to send out his disciples in twos to preach his message and warn the people to repent. They also, apparently, found that they were performing miracles. So the mission of Jesus was going well at this point (except in Nazareth!). But the mission of his forerunner, John the Baptist, had come to an end.

Mark tells the story as a flashback, arising from King Herod's fear that Jesus was a reincarnation of John. Herod had arrested John because of his public condemnation of Herod's marriage to his brother's wife, Herodias. But he would probably not have dared to execute John, who was highly regarded as a prophet.

His hand was forced by Herodias' daughter, who is usually known as Salome (though unnamed in the Gospels), in the way described here by Mark. It's a classic case of an unwise vow with dire consequences—and also of the danger of putting your own dignity above justice (see verse 26).

So John the Baptist was beheaded, and his disciples took away his body and buried it.

King Herod

The Herods were puppet rulers who were only able to retain their position by the backing of the hated Roman occupiers. The ancient lands of Israel had been under Greek and then Roman occupation for about 300 years, and were now divided into several provinces, of which Galilee was one. The King Herod who was on the throne at the time of the birth of Jesus (see Matthew 2:1) was Herod the Great, who was 'king of the Jews'. He was succeeded by his son, Archelaus, who was deposed by the Romans after two years. The next Herod, Antipas, was ruler only of the Galilean and Peraean parts of the kingdom (the northern and eastern parts). He was the ruler of Galilee during the ministry of Jesus and ordered the beheading of John the Baptist.

Mark 6:30-56
Two miracles with one message

This passage relates in detail two apparently very different miracles: feeding 5,000 men with loaves and fish, and Jesus walking on the water. It ends with a picture of Jesus healing large numbers of people in the streets of Gennesaret. At the end of the accounts of the first two miracles, when the disciples were 'completely amazed' by the walking on the water, Mark comments that this was because 'they had not understood the real meaning of the feeding of the five thousand; their minds could not grasp it'. So clearly the clue to them both lies in the story of the bread and fish.

This miracle is the only one recorded in all four Gospels, so obviously it was seen as very important and significant by the first Christians. Not only that, but the vivid detail of the story—the crowd, the conversation with the disciples, the explicit instructions about precisely how the food was to be distributed—makes you feel that there is 'more in this than meets the eye'! And you would be right.

Let's start by saying that clearly something very remarkable happened at that 'lonely place' not far from the lake. The popularity of the story, the details which have an eyewitness quality about them, and the importance which the Gospels give to it, suggest a truly memorable occurrence. So those critics—mostly in the past—who tried to rationalize the story were surely wide of the mark. This was not just an exercise in communal sandwich sharing, as some of them suggested!

For the first Christians the significance of the story was

that Jesus cared for his followers when they needed it. Indeed, by his own power and authority he met their needs. When they felt alone, weak and powerless, Jesus the Son of God fed them in the desert, just as God had fed the Israelites with manna on their journey through the desert long ago (you can read about it in Exodus chapter 16).

Not only that, but the early Christians saw in this story a model for what they experienced every week in the 'breaking of bread'—what we call the eucharist, or holy communion. Jesus took bread, blessed it, broke it and gave it to his apostles to distribute—just as their leaders took bread in the name of Jesus, blessed and broke it and distributed it to them Sunday by Sunday. The miracle is about Jesus meeting the needs of his people. The message is that he still does.

And so is the miracle of the 'walking on water', if only they could see it. The disciples were facing mountainous difficulties—they were 'straining at the oars, the wind was against them'. But Jesus came to them, walking across the water—the 'waters' which, in the Old Testament, often represent times of testing. He spoke words of courage to them, and climbed into the boat alongside them. Again, he met their need—not for food, this time, but for security and protection. In the times of persecution that lay ahead for the Church, it's not surprising that they valued these two stories of Jesus meeting all the needs of his people—in the desert, and facing contrary winds and high seas!

Mark 7 : 1 – 2 3
Clean—and unclean

We've already seen that Jesus had a radically new approach
to religious matters—a way that clashed sharply with the
traditions of the time. Here we read of a confrontation
between Jesus and the Pharisees and 'teachers of the Law'.

They were worried that some of the disciples of Jesus
weren't fulfilling the proper traditions before they ate their
food. This involved a ritual hand-washing, not for hygienic
reasons, but religious ones. It also involved the ritual
washing of the pots, cups and bowls which they were to
use. Presumably the disciples had already realized that
Jesus didn't put much store by such practices, and had
quietly let them lapse. Now the eagle eyes of the religious
'Thought Police' were on them!

But Jesus came to their defence. He didn't argue about
the specific rituals that were in question, but attacked the
whole principle of putting outward ceremonies above
inward truth. He quoted the prophet Isaiah to them,
accusing the people of his day of honouring God with their
lips while their hearts were in rebellion against him. In
other words, it's what you are inside that matters, not
what you do on the outside.

He then took the attack to their own practices. He
accused the religious teachers of hypocrisy (verse 6—it
simply means 'play-acting'). They cleverly got around the
true demands of God's Law while keeping up the
'traditions'. So the Law of God says that we should 'honour
our fathers and mothers' (verse 10), but they had worked

out a method of avoiding the practical implications of this. If they designated money that should have gone to support their parents as 'Corban' (it means 'a gift to God'), then they were excused from giving it to them. In that way, they kept the letter of the Law but broke its spirit.

Jesus then set out what he taught as the principle at stake here. Things that come to us from outside—like ritual uncleanness, and the various foods that they were forbidden to eat by religious Law—can't do us any real harm. Evil comes from inside, from an evil heart, from bad motives and desires.

So Jesus made the inwardness of true religion into a principle. His followers should seek for pure hearts, rather than clean hands!

The Pharisees

The Pharisees don't on the whole emerge with a lot of credit from the Gospels, which is probably unfair on them. The reason that they took the brunt of Jesus' attacks on the teachers of the Law was that at this period they were the dominant religious group. They believed they had simplified the Law, reducing it to 365 negative commands and 248 positive ones! For example, there were thirty-nine prohibited kinds of activity on the sabbath. They were very keen on tithing (giving a tenth of one's income to God) and emphasized that each individual had a duty to fulfil the Law—as compared to their rivals, the Sadducees, who put more stress on temple worship. The Pharisees, like Jesus, believed in the resurrection of the dead—again, in contrast to the Sadducees.

17

Mark 7:24–37
A Gentile healed

This incident happened on the coast at Tyre, which was then in the province of Phoenicia—nowadays it would be in Lebanon. It was largely a Gentile area, though many Jews also lived there. Jesus wanted to have some privacy, but this Gentile woman came to him and begged him to heal her daughter.

The reply of Jesus seems surprising, even rude, but that's largely because we think of 'dog' as an insult. In fact, what Jesus was saying was this his mission was to the 'lost sheep of the house of Israel', and at this point he had to concentrate on offering the children of God's promise, the Jews, the good news before it could be offered to anyone else.

He may have said this to test her faith. At any rate, she responded in a forthright way. Even dogs can eat the leftovers!

Jesus was pleased with her answer: it showed both faith and insight—that quality of openness that marks the good soil in which the seed of his message could grow. And he healed her daughter.

The second healing here is of a deaf and dumb man. One of the great prophecies of the Messiah—God's promised deliverer—was that the ears of the deaf would be opened and the tongue of the dumb shout for joy (see Isaiah 35:5).

The people would have known this, which may explain their amazement and awe. After all, if he caused the deaf to hear and the dumb to speak the kingdom of God must have arrived!

As so often, Jesus told them not to speak of it to anyone, but they simply took no notice!

18

Mark 8 : 1 – 26
Miracles—but not to order!

Here we have another story of miraculous feeding. Virtually the only difference from the earlier account is the numbers involved—slightly more bread, slightly fewer people! Some experts think that this is simply another account of the same event, but obviously Mark didn't think so, or he wouldn't have included it in his Gospel. In both stories one of the key phrases seems to be, 'Everybody ate and had enough'—these are stories of Jesus satisfying his children, not just giving them the bare minimum.

The feeding story is followed by the little scene in which some Pharisees try to trap Jesus by asking him to perform a miracle to authenticate his ministry. This is almost exactly one of the temptations which Jesus faced after his baptism, during his time in the desert (you can read about it in Luke 4:1–13)—to perform a miracle so that everyone would believe he was the Son of God. He rejected it then, and he rejected it now. He wasn't in the business of providing proof. Faith was what he looked for.

This scene is followed by one between Jesus and the disciples. They hadn't brought enough bread with them, and Jesus took the opportunity to warn them about what he called the 'yeast' of the Pharisees. Yeast was an essential ingredient in the baking of ordinary bread, but at Passover time the Jews abstained from yeast and every trace of it was carefully removed from their homes. So yeast became a byword for traces of sin, which left untreated would grow into big ones!

The Pharisees—and Herod, the evil king—were like yeast in that they wormed their way into people's lives and into the religious life of the time with every appearance of goodness. But actually they were a destructive force.

The disciples, not for the first time, got entirely the wrong end of the stick. They thought Jesus was complaining about their failure to bring enough bread (goodness knows how they arrived at that!). So again he chided them for having closed eyes and closed minds. They had just seen the miracle of the loaves, yet they couldn't understand that he would meet all of their needs if only they would trust him.

The healing of the blind man at Bethsaida, by Galilee, is unusual in that it took place in two stages. At first he saw, but with distorted vision. Then, when Jesus placed his hands on him a second time, he saw clearly. It's probably not being too fanciful to suggest that Mark recorded this incident to remind his hearers that Christ's work in us isn't always instant—sometimes we need a second (or third, or hundredth) touch of his hand to be made whole.

19

Mark 8:27 — 9:1
The turning point

Mark's story has now reached a crucial point. It is about eighteen months since the baptism of Jesus, and the prophet from Galilee has achieved an enormous reputation in that time, both as healer and teacher. Huge crowds have flocked to hear him and to ask for cures. The religious leaders have come down from 'headquarters' in Jerusalem to check on him, and have decided that he is an enemy of the present system. And the disciples—a collection of fishermen, country-folk and one former tax collector— have watched all this in some astonishment. They have seen the miracles. They have heard the parables. They have lived with this strange, powerful but gentle man day and night. What have they made of it?

And now, as they were walking on a long, hot journey through the northern villages near Caesarea Philippi, Jesus put the question to them. First he asked who 'people' say he is: that's quite easy, and the answers fell over each other. 'But what about you? Who do you say that I am?'

Obviously this question didn't require the answer 'Jesus of Nazareth', and they knew what he meant. Having watched and observed and been involved in all he had done since his public ministry began, were they now able to decide who he is?

Peter presumably answered for them all: 'You are the Messiah'. It was a brief answer—much briefer than the version given in the other Gospels—but it said everything. For a devout Jew like Peter, it was an earth-shattering confession. The man with whom they had shared the last eighteen months—sleeping rough, walking the lanes, staying in this village and that—was none other than the saviour and deliverer promised by God for countless centuries. History—at any rate, Jewish history—had found its culmination in this Galilean from Nazareth.

It is no exaggeration to say that this is the turning point in Mark's Gospel. From this moment on the whole mood changes. The disciples have come to grasp the truth about Jesus and the period of first awakening their faith in him and opening their eyes to his true identity is over. From now on a more sombre mood dominates the ministry of Jesus. The path through Galilee turns into the road to Jerusalem, and the road to Jerusalem leads to death.

And that is the point Jesus now made to his followers. They may have thought that being the disciples of the Messiah would be a glory trip. Far from it. What lay ahead was suffering, rejection, self-denial and death... to be followed by 'rising to life'.

Peter objected to this grim scenario, and earned a rebuke from Jesus. These objections were not from God, but from the adversary, Satan. If anyone was to follow Jesus, they must face the fact that it would be a costly, self-sacrificial path—but also a path that led to 'life'.

And Jesus added a strange promise. 'Some of them' would see the kingdom of God come with power before they died.

20

Mark 9 : 2 – 13

Glory on the mountain

The connecting words 'six days later' are important. Such detail is rare in Mark. He probably wanted to connect what follows with what had gone immediately before, both the disciples' confession of faith in Jesus as Messiah and the promise of Jesus that 'some of them' would see the 'kingdom of God' before they died. Now 'some of them'— Peter, James and John, to be precise—were to be given a unique and unforgettable privilege: they were to get a glimpse of Jesus in the glory of heaven.

He took them up a 'high mountain' and there, before their eyes, he was changed—the usual translation 'transfigured' conveys the real meaning rather better. There was a glowing white brightness about Jesus, and two figures also appeared in this vision, whom the disciples took to be Elijah (the great father of the prophets of Israel) and Moses (the giver of the Law). So the 'Law and the Prophets' were fulfilled in Jesus.

Peter (who 'didn't know what to say', but was incapable of staying silent!) offered to erect three tents for them to stay in, as though this marvellous vision could be trapped and kept permanently.

Then they heard a voice from the sky saying, 'This is my Son—listen to him.' And with that the vision disappeared, leaving just Jesus with the three astonished men.

On the way down the hill they were warned not to talk about this until after the resurrection of Jesus, but they still couldn't resist discussing it among themselves. Their question about Elijah showed that they understood the meaning of what they had just seen. Jewish tradition said that Elijah would return before the Messiah came—a tradition still marked at every Passover by the presence of a cup of wine for Elijah, should he come. They were convinced that Jesus was the Messiah, both as a matter of faith and, now, of confirmation through this vision. But where was Elijah? Why hadn't he come first?

The reply of Jesus was that Elijah had already come, and had been badly treated—almost certainly a reference to John the Baptist, who is identified with Elijah in Luke's Gospel (1:17).

At any rate, from this time on the central core of the disciples, Peter, James and John, would never again doubt that Jesus was the Messiah. And this vision on the mountain would never leave their memories: 'we saw his glory', says John in his Gospel (1:14).

Messiah

For centuries the Jewish people had been expecting the coming of their 'Messiah'. The word in Hebrew means 'Anointed One'. It often appears in the New Testament in its Greek equivalent, 'Christ'. At different times in their history, from Moses—1,000 years before Jesus—to the great prophets of the exile in the sixth and seventh centuries BC, there were prophecies that God would send this great saviour and deliverer to rescue and restore his people. By the time of Jesus, after 300 years of enemy occupation, the hope of the coming of the Messiah had reached desperation pitch. There had been many false 'messiahs', and there were also religious groups who warned that the Messiah would not come until the religious life of Israel was reformed.

Most people thought of the 'Messiah' as some kind of conquering king (hence the 'anointed'), although certainly some of Isaiah's prophecies suggested a suffering saviour of a quite different kind (see Isaiah 53). Even the disciples were slow to appreciate that Jesus was a Messiah who would suffer for his people, rather than overthrow the present corrupt rulers and take over the throne of Israel.

21

Mark 9 : 14 – 3 2
Faith and healing

As so often in life, the wonderful experience on the mountain top was immediately followed by a crashing return to earth! When Jesus and the three others joined the rest of the disciples they found a desperately sad situation had developed. A man had brought his son to the disciples for healing. From the description of his symptoms, it seems that he had a severe epileptic condition. The father, in line with contemporary ideas, assumed the boy was possessed, and had asked the disciples to exorcise the evil spirit, but they had failed. Somehow the 'teachers of the Law' had also got involved, and a large crowd had gathered.

Jesus saw the whole miserable situation as a consequence of unbelief—even on the part of the disciples, it would seem. 'Bring the boy to me.'

The boy immediately fell into a fit. The father confirmed that this was a condition he had had since childhood, and begged for help from Jesus—if he possibly could.

The reply of Jesus is unusual. The issue was not whether Jesus could heal the boy, but whether the father could believe. 'Everything is possible for the person who has faith.'

The father's reply is honest and desperate. Yes, he did have faith, but not enough for this. Couldn't Jesus help him to have more faith? It is a prayer many of us must have felt like praying in various situations.

Jesus responded by healing the boy, in a dramatic

sequence of events. After it was all over, the disciples asked why they couldn't do what he had done. The answer of Jesus was enigmatic in the extreme: 'Only prayer can drive this kind out'. One supposes they had prayed. One also supposes that Jesus was referring to a kind of believing prayer that makes 'everything possible', and which was, at that stage, beyond their experience.

The remaining verses of this section are very revealing. Jesus now wanted to concentrate on teaching his disciples. Perhaps the crowds had had their opportunity to believe in him through the miracles and signs he had offered them. Certainly Mark has very few more to relate—and we have already seen the last exorcism in the Gospel. Now was the time for the Twelve to be initiated into that 'mystery' that had been kept secret from blind eyes and closed minds, the mystery of a Messiah who would suffer for the people, but rise from the dead. It was not a 'secret' which the disciples found easy either to accept or to understand.

22

Mark 9:33–50
Dealing with temptation

It's depressing, but typical, that the first reaction of the disciples to this call to understand the need for self-sacrifice and suffering was to squabble about which of them was the 'greatest'. I suppose they meant, 'What's the pecking order in the group?' For answer, Jesus offered a visual aid—a small child. God would be honoured if they were to honour a small child—someone with no 'status' at all. The highest place would go to the humblest—the one who was prepared to 'serve' all the others. It's another example of the values of the kingdom of heaven turning the world's values upside down.

The disciples had another lesson to learn, too. The new 'kingdom' would include all sorts of people they didn't entirely approve of—people who 'don't belong to our group', but who, however misguidedly, act 'in the name of Jesus'. Such a person is positive about the kingdom—for it, not against it—and should be welcomed. So Jesus set his face against what we call 'sectarianism' in the new community—a 'them-and-us' attitude that has wrecked many churches and often given Christianity a bad name.

On the other hand, while people whose beliefs may not precisely coincide with ours are to be welcomed if they name the name of Christ, those who wilfully sin are to be rejected. Offences against 'little ones' are given first place, but the general drift of what Jesus is teaching here is that rejecting evil is an absolute priority, to be pursued whatever the cost—it is worth more than a limb or an eye, even.

The penalty for evil persisted in is 'hell'—not, in this case, the eternal torment portrayed in medieval paintings, but the purifying fires of the city rubbish dumps. 'Gehenna' (the word Jesus used here) was the name for the valley just outside Jerusalem where the city's rubbish was burnt, and its fires glowed and smoked day and night—and what the fires missed, the worms consumed! So the 'hell' Jesus was speaking of was a purifying fire, that got rid of evil and corruption, rather than a place of punishment. Verse 49 makes the point very clearly: 'Everyone will be purified by fire.'

'Salt' was vital in the ancient world, a purifying agent, rather like fire. The disciples of Jesus needed to be well 'salted' to keep pure in a corrupting world—and to support each other in lives of peace and goodness (verse 50).

This teaching of Jesus isn't easy and perhaps it's not very congenial to modern ears. Yet evil exists—we all know it does. And evil must be fought with the proper weapons. For Jesus those weapons were the weapons of the kingdom: a holy life, a proper sense of priorities, and a humble faith in God, like the simple trust of a child.

Mark 10:1–16
Divorce—and children

As part of their plan to entrap Jesus, the Pharisees would approach him with questions which they hoped would place him in a difficult position. Here is a typical example. They knew perfectly well what the Law of Moses said about divorce, but they also knew that Jesus liked to get behind the literal wording of a law and teach the principle that underlay it. So they expected that he would not simply endorse what the Law said, which was that a man could divorce his wife by issuing a simple notice sending her away. There was a dispute at that time between those who claimed the Law only allowed him to do that when she had done something indecent, or simply if she 'displeased' him.

Jesus had a higher view of marriage than that, and therefore a stricter view on divorce. For him, marriage was instituted by God to unite one man to one woman for life. Human laws should not undo what God had joined together. In this case, too, Jesus was getting behind the practice, which was to meet the needs of fallible and weak human beings, to the principle, which was of a lifelong union.

In contrast to this apparently 'tough' line on divorce, Jesus treated the children and their mothers very gently. When the disciples tried to send them away, presumably because Jesus was too tired or busy to see them, he was angry with them. 'Let the children come to me... because the kingdom of God belongs to such as these'. Only those with a childlike trust in God could really understand what his kingdom is all about.

Mark 10:17–31
A rich man and Jesus

The man who accosted Jesus in this story was, we read, 'very rich'. That is the clue to the whole story! He was obviously also very religious—he wanted to know how to receive eternal life, he had kept all the commandments from his youth and he called Jesus 'Good Teacher'. But Jesus asked from him the one thing which he couldn't bring himself to surrender—his wealth. Although it made him sad to do it, he went away from Jesus rather than part with the possessions that gave him power and status.

The story leads to the famous remark of Jesus that it is harder for a rich person to enter the kingdom of God than for a camel to go through the eye of a needle.

Yet Jesus met other wealthy people—like Nicodemus (John 3) and Joseph of Arimathea (John 19:38)—and welcomed them as his followers without demanding that they gave away all their wealth.

Clearly there was something which Jesus saw in this particular rich man which told him that while he retained his wealth he would never truly follow Jesus. Although Jesus looked at him with 'love' (verse 21), he knew a fatal weakness when he saw one! The general remark about the camel and the needle simply underlines the principle: wealth, possessions, 'things' are extra weights on the journey of faith, and we must be prepared to shed them if necessary. For this man it was necessary; for Nicodemus and Joseph it wasn't.

There's one other small but important point. Why did

Jesus seem to correct him when he called him 'Good Teacher'—'No one is good except God alone'? Wasn't Jesus divine? Couldn't the Son of God also be called 'good'? What was the point of this apparently scrupulous correction?

The simplest, and therefore probably correct, answer is that Jesus was inviting him to think carefully about what he was saying. To call a teacher 'good' was to put him on a level with God. Was that what the rich man intended? And 'goodness' was tested by the commandments, which represent God's standards. Perhaps Jesus found his approach to him rather too flattering, and wanted to test his sincerity right from the start.

After this encounter, the disciples were quick to apply it to themselves, in a slightly self-righteous way. 'We've given up everything for you, so we'll be all right, won't we?' Jesus agreed that, in principle, those who gave up anything for his sake would be generously rewarded—though the rewards included the stinging addition 'and persecutions as well'! Eternal life would be theirs, too—but only if they remembered that persistent theme of the teaching of Jesus: the first will be last, and the last first. God has a preference for the poor and weak, and resists the proud and powerful. It was a lesson that sent the rich man away, but the disciples, to their credit, stayed with him.

25

Mark 10:32–52

Two brothers and a blind man

Jesus had now turned his face towards Jerusalem—a prospect which filled the disciples with alarm. They felt reasonably safe in their home district of Galilee, where Jesus was very popular. But they had seen the sinister officials from Jerusalem mingling with the crowds and asking incriminating questions. They had heard Jesus' own dire predictions of what lay ahead of him in the capital. Now they heard them again, for a third time. No wonder they hung back as he strode ahead!

All of which makes it even more surprising that James and John, the sons of Zebedee, and two of the favoured inner core of disciples, should come to him with this audacious request. At least they believed there was going to be a 'glorious Kingdom'... but then, they had seen Jesus in his glory on the mountain. But could they be assured of the top places when that kingdom arrived—one in the chief place of honour, on his right, and the other in the second place, on his left?

Jesus answered with a gentle rebuke. They didn't understand what they were requesting. Were they prepared to share his 'cup' (that is, the bitterness of his suffering) and his 'baptism' (that is, the death he was to face)?

Possibly they didn't understand the full implication of his question. At any rate, they said they could and would. And Jesus agreed, they would one day share his suffering and even his death—James was martyred for his faith, John exiled in his old age. But they could not demand places which only God could fill, and he had already made his choice. Jesus may have been referring to the criminals who would share his crucifixion (one on the right, and the other on the left).

When the other disciples heard about this conversation they were furious with James and John. So Jesus gave them all a lecture on the difference between the values of his kingdom and earthly values. On earth, leaders and rulers lord it over people, enjoying the opportunity to exercise power. 'This, however, is not the way it is among you'. In the kingdom of heaven, the great must be servants, the leader must be the slave of all.

Why, even Jesus, the 'Son of Man', didn't come to 'lord' it, but to serve—and to give his life to rescue people from death.

On their way to Jerusalem they passed through the ancient city of Jericho, where Jesus healed a blind man called Bartimaeus. There now seemed to be no need for secrecy—Bartimaeus was not told to keep his healing to himself—in fact, he followed Jesus towards Jerusalem. But again the 'faith' theme is stressed: 'your faith has made you well'.

Son of Man

This is the way Jesus often referred to himself. It's a title from the Old Testament, from the book of Daniel (see Daniel 7:13–14), where it refers to a heavenly figure in human form who was given authority, glory and power, and a 'kingdom that will never be destroyed'. It is also used elsewhere to mean simply a 'human being', usually in a representative way—'The Man', we might say.

When Jesus used the title he was certainly giving it a deeper significance than simply 'human being'. The connection with the prophecy in Daniel would have been an obvious one to his hearers, and they would have deduced from that that he was a human figure with divine authority. I imagine that is exactly what he intended the title to convey.

26

Mark 11:1–19
Palm Sunday

Now Jesus and his disciples had reached Jerusalem, the sacred city of the Jews, where the magnificent temple stood in all its glory. As they came up from Jericho they approached the city from the east, past Bethphage and Bethany, and came to the Mount of Olives, which faces the temple mount. Here Jesus sent some of the disciples off to acquire the colt on which he would ride down the hill and into the city.

As Jesus made his way down the steep slope, the disciples who had come with him from Galilee were perhaps joined by others in giving him a hero's welcome. Branches were laid in his path, and even people's cloaks, and the cry went up 'Hosanna!—God bless him who comes in the name of the Lord! God bless the coming kingdom of David...' It was a royal welcome—a welcome for the Messiah, no less.

Jesus knew the prophecy of Zechariah about the coming Messiah, which spoke of their 'king coming, righteous and having salvation, gentle and riding on a donkey'. It was no accident, then, that he entered in this way—and the disciples responded to the gesture. Surely, they must have thought, this is the moment: the Messiah is here, he has announced his arrival in the Holy City, and will surely now take power and assume the kingdom, as God had promised. So this last week in Jerusalem began on a high note—perhaps a dangerously high one.

Jesus and the twelve disciples were staying at Bethany,

on the outskirts of Jerusalem. As they made their way into the city the next day, the incident with the fig tree occurred. As it is rather a strange one, we may assume there is, once again, more to it than meets the eye.

Many times in the Old Testament Israel—the people of God of the 'old' covenant—are likened to a fig tree. They were meant to 'bear fruit' to God's glory. But this fig tree on the path to Jerusalem had plenty of leaves, but no fruit—leading Jesus to say that it would never bear fruit again.

Israel's moment of judgment had come, with the arrival of the Messiah, Jesus, in Jerusalem. But already Jesus knew that he was going to be rejected. Their religion, you might say, was too much leaf and not enough fruit—too much outward show and not enough inward reality. So they would miss out on the harvest.

If we see this incident as a kind of acted parable, it provides a vivid pointer to much of what happened in this last week leading up to Good Friday. The 'old' religion was facing its moment of decision. It was under judgment. If it rejected the Messiah, either through ignorance or ill-will, then it faced a truly barren future.

The dramatic events in the temple are also part of this process of judgment. Jesus saw the merchants and money-changers operating within the temple precincts as a blasphemy. Its main purpose was prayer, not profit! So, in a moment of holy outrage, he literally drove them out. So much for 'Gentle Jesus, meek and mild'!

27

Mark 11:20—12:12
Confronting the opposition

When Jesus and his disciples walked into the city the next morning, they noticed that the fig tree had died. In terms of the acted parable, that spoke of the death of the 'old' order. But Jesus also used it to call his disciples to greater faith, for that was the absolute heart of the 'new' order— that, and forgiveness, the essential companion of true prayer.

When they reached the temple, the first of several confrontations with the religious authorities took place. Jesus was asked about the source of his authority. Where did it come from? It certainly had not come from the temple leadership. He was not an authorized rabbi (teacher). He was not a lawyer or a priest. How dare an ordinary lay person, without any special training or education, assume such authority?

Jesus, in true Jewish style, answered a question with a question. Where did John the Baptist get his authority from? (After all, he too was an unauthorized lay person.)

This led to some confusion. If they agreed that John's authority came directly from God (which was what 'everyone' believed), then Jesus would ask why they didn't follow John's advice and become his disciples. If they said his authority was merely human, the people would turn against them. So, wisely, they said they couldn't answer. To which Jesus responded that he wouldn't answer their question, either.

The story of the tenants in the vineyard picks up again

the theme of Israel and its rejection of Jesus as Messiah. I've said that Israel was often compared to a fig tree; even more often, it was called a vine—God's vine. And he looked for good fruit from it.

The parable develops that idea. When the time for the grape harvest came, God sent various of his servants to collect from the tenants of the vineyard his share of the produce. These servants are, presumably, the prophets of Israel and John the Baptist. Each was rejected, often being shamefully treated and even killed. Eventually the owner sent his own son, thinking they would respect him. But in fact they killed him and threw his body out of the vineyard.

The judgment on the tenants of the vineyard—the religious leaders of Jesus' time, we must assume—was severe. The vineyard would be taken from them and given to 'other tenants'. What they had rejected as worthless would become precious to others.

No wonder the Jewish leaders decided that this parable was aimed at them. It simply increased their determination to arrest Jesus, if they could find a way to do it without inciting the crowd.

28

Mark 12:13-44
Question time

With Jesus teaching every day in the temple area, the religious leaders were able to subject him to an unending barrage of tricky questions. They were, of course, trying to find suitable evidence to use against him in the trial which, they hoped, would follow his imminent arrest. Here Mark gives us three such questions.

First, what about taxes to the hated Romans? Should we pay them, or not? The answer 'Yes' would alienate the public; the answer 'No' would incur the wrath of the Roman authorities.

The response of Jesus was to ask someone to hand him a coin. Whose image was on it (whose 'face and name')? 'The emperor's', they had to reply—Tiberius Caesar, at that time.

The reply of Jesus put the whole discussion on a different plane. They should give to Caesar what bore Caesar's image, and to God what bore God's image. The coin bore the image of Caesar—he had issued it and it signified his rule. But what bore the image of God? What was 'issued' by him and signifies his rule? The answer can only be every human being. We are all made 'in the image of God', are his creatures and are only true to our nature when we live under his rule. No one could dispute the logic of this—in fact, 'they were amazed at Jesus'.

Secondly, there is an even more complicated question about the resurrection of the dead. This was put to Jesus by members of the Sadducee party. They were the great rivals of the Pharisees. Unlike the Pharisees, they didn't believe in the resurrection of the dead.

Their question was designed to show how ridiculous the whole idea of resurrection was. If a woman during her life was married to seven men—all brothers, who were bound by Law to marry their brother's widow—whose wife would she be on the day of resurrection? It's the sort of question some people still raise to try to ridicule the idea of life beyond death.

Jesus' answer was that they had a completely wrong idea of what resurrection life would be like. Questions such as who was married to whom would be irrelevant in the life of heaven—as would jealousy, possessiveness and exclusivity. It wouldn't be just an extension of the kind of life we know now—to think that is to misunderstand 'God's power'.

But he had a stronger point, about the principle at stake, which was that of the dead rising to life. He referred them to one of the best known stories in their scriptures: Moses at the burning bush (Exodus 3:6). When God spoke to Moses he called himself 'the God of Abraham, Isaac and Jacob'—people who were already long dead. So clearly they still existed, or he couldn't be their 'God'! 'He is the God of the living, not of the dead.'

The third question—perhaps a more genuine one—came from another teacher of the Law who asked Jesus which was the most important commandment. Jesus replied that the most important one was to love God, and the next most important was to love our neighbour. These were the basis of all moral law.

The religious teacher didn't disagree. Indeed, he complimented Jesus on his answer—and received a compliment in return: 'You are not far from the kingdom of God'.

Compliments from Jesus at this stage were two-edged weapons, and from then on no one dared ask him any more questions.

However, Jesus himself had one or two left to ask! One was to enquire about the relationship of the Messiah to David, the great king of Israel. It was commonly believed that the Messiah would be a 'son' (that is, descendant) of David—which, according to the New Testament, Jesus in fact was.

But he had a more important point to make. David, in one of his Psalms, spoke of the Messiah as his 'Lord'—so how could he be his son? The Messiah would be greater than David.

Despite their constant presence, Jesus did not modify his criticisms of the teachers of the Law. Here (verses 38–40) he accuses them of hypocrisy—'walking about in long robes… [but taking] advantage of widows and robbing them of their houses'. Hypocrisy—acting a religious role while living a lie—is the worst of all sins for Jesus, which put these teachers in a very bad position!

The passage ends with a sharp contrast—the poor widow who gave her last two copper coins to God. This, for Jesus, is true religion, not play-acting. She didn't give to God what was left over after she had met all her own wants: 'she gave all she had'.

29

Mark 13:1–36
A vision of the future

Let's admit right away that this is a very difficult passage! Whole books have been written in an attempt to uncover its meaning and to unravel the various strands that seem to make up a very complicated answer to a quite straightforward question. The disciples, having heard Jesus say that one day the great temple—one of the outstanding buildings of the ancient world—would be destroyed, asked him 'when this will be'. The long discourse which follows is offered by Mark as his answer.

Various problems face a modern reader as they go through this chapter. The biggest of them is that it is written in a literary form that was common—and indeed very popular—at the time of Jesus, but is foreign to us. It is known as an apocalypse, which is from a Greek word meaning 'revelation' or 'unveiling'.

Usually apocalyptic writings were full of colourful visions and vivid language, purporting to predict the future but also to show that whatever happened was within some kind of overriding plan and purpose. The most obvious example in the Bible is the book of Revelation, at the end of the New Testament, where the writer, John, recounts a series of visions about the future. But there is also some vivid apocalyptic writing in the book of Daniel, in the Old Testament, some of which is incorporated in the language of this discourse.

An 'apocalypse' is not like the writings of Nostradamus, or modern fantasy fiction about the future, though sometimes it reads rather like it! An apocalypse has a purpose, and that is to reassure its readers that things don't happen by accident. Horrible as they may be, they are part of a larger purpose.

This chapter is placed by Mark after the events following Palm Sunday, but before the arrest, trial and crucifixion of Jesus, probably to make that very point. These events, as you read them, may look like the triumph of evil over good. But you would be wrong! Behind them all, and far into the future, God has a greater purpose. He is working to a long agenda, not based on instant solutions. So, armed with this understanding, we can go ahead to read of the terrible events of Good Friday without feeling that God has been defeated.

Having said all that, the chapter still presents problems. It seems most unlikely that Jesus said all of these things in one speech, and in precisely this order. Indeed, one biblical scholar, T.W. Manson, has suggested that verses 32–37 are probably the original answer of Jesus to the question put by the disciples, and that the rest of the chapter is a gathering together by Mark of various other things that Jesus said about the future of Jerusalem, the judgment on the Jewish people, the times of testing that lay ahead for the Christians, and the 'Day of the Lord', which is to all intents and purposes the same thing as the 'end of the world'.

Because Mark has gathered them in sections, it's impossible to build from this chapter a coherent pattern of prophecy about future events, and those who have tried to do so have invariably got it wrong!

What we can see is that awful events lay ahead for the Jewish people, and these certainly did happen—Jerusalem was burnt to the ground and the temple destroyed in AD70, and many Jews were scattered all over the ancient world. 'The Awful Horror' (verse 14) probably refers to the desecration of the temple.

It's also a fact that terrible persecution lay ahead for the Christian Church—persecutions that began before AD70 and went on spasmodically for well over 200 years. This was mostly, of course, at the hands of the Romans. Millions of Christians were arrested, executed, killed in the arena or fed to the lions. Verses 9–13 seem to be dealing with events of this kind.

The passage on the coming of the Son of man (verses 24–27 and 32–37) deals with the ultimate future. It looks on to the 'Day of the Lord', which for the Jews was the great day of God's judgment. Jesus identified this with his own return to earth 'with great power and glory' (verse 26). But he warned his hearers not to speculate about when it would happen—no one but God the Father knows the day or hour when it will take place, not the angels and not even the Son of God. It's strange, in the light of this warning, that some Christians have always been ready to tell us when they think it will be!

I expect a first reading of this chapter left you highly confused! For most of us, the best way to approach it is not to worry about the details, but to let the images and pictures wash over us, while absorbing their one main message: through all the dark and painful events that mark human history, there is a golden thread of God's purpose. It is not just chaos. Evil does not triumph in the end. As the hymn puts it, 'God is working his purpose out, as year succeeds to year'.

And the end of everything will be centred on the Son of man himself, the very person we have seen healing and comforting and forgiving and overcoming evil on his journey from Galilee to Jerusalem. He is the one to whom the Father has delegated final judgment. I hope you find that as encouraging an idea as the Christians did for whom Mark first wrote these words nearly 2,000 years ago.

30

Mark 14:1-11
Something beautiful at Bethany

We have now reached Wednesday. The great festival of Passover lay just two days ahead. Jesus and his disciples were still staying overnight at Bethany, and spending their days in the city. On this occasion they were having a meal at the house of a man called Simon, who had been a 'leper'—he had suffered from the terrible skin condition that drove people out of human society. Obviously he was now clear of the disease, so perhaps Jesus had healed him.

According to the practice of the time, the guests would have been lying on couches around the low table. As they were eating, this unusual event took place. The jar of perfume was probably intended for burial rites and may have been kept in someone's family for that purpose. It was certainly very valuable—according to the astonished bystanders it was worth 300 silver coins, which in modern currency would be something like £4,000. At any rate, it all ended up anointing the head of Jesus—and probably filling the whole house with its perfume.

It's not surprising that people criticized what they would see as 'waste', but Jesus didn't agree. He said that the woman had done 'a fine and beautiful thing' for him—she had prepared him 'ahead of time' for his burial. Not many people get to smell the embalming oils for their own body!

Mark doesn't say who the woman was. It is at least possible (from similar stories in the other Gospels) that she was Mary of Magdala, a follower of Jesus who had been delivered by him from evil possession. Whether that is so or not, her gesture, said Jesus, would be recounted wherever the good news was preached all over the world—and by putting the story in his Gospel, Mark has made the prophecy come true.

This act of extravagant devotion may have been the last straw for one of the disciples, Judas Iscariot. Perhaps he had been anxious for some time about the way things were going. He had agreed to follow a kingly Messiah, not a powerless prophet who was going to be executed by the authorities. Perhaps he didn't like all this talk of being delivered into the hands of wicked men and crucified. This simple gesture of anointing, with the remark of Jesus about being prepared for his burial, may have struck him as sheer defeatism.

Whatever the reason, he had clearly had enough, and went off to the 'chief priests' at the temple to offer to help them arrest Jesus. They offered him money (which may or may not have been an important factor), and in return he would look out for a suitable opportunity for the capture of Jesus at a time when it wouldn't provoke a public riot.

Mark carefully describes him as 'one of the twelve disciples'. I suppose it is simply that that has made his betrayal so appalling, and his name throughout subsequent history a byword for the worst kind of disloyalty.

Passover

'Passover' is a Jewish festival which commemorates the freeing of the Hebrew slaves from Egypt under the leadership of Moses, roughly 1,000 years before Christ. Their forefathers had gone to Egypt in a time of famine, but they were eventually enslaved and put to building treasure stores by the Egyptian kings (Pharaohs). God called Moses to be the human agent of their freedom, the final step of which was a plague in which the firstborn sons of Egypt were to be struck dead in one night of disaster. In order to avoid this fate, the Hebrews (Jews) were to kill a lamb, eat it, and smear its blood on their doorposts. Then the 'angel of death' would 'pass over' their homes, leaving them unscathed. The plague did indeed lead to their release, and, as commanded by God, they re-created that final 'pass-over' meal every year on its anniversary, as a memorial of God's mercy to them.

In the time of Jesus the Passover was the greatest festival in the Jewish calendar, lasting several days, and it was at the Passover feast that he met his death. Jews the world over still celebrate Passover, which usually coincides (for obvious reasons) with the Christian Holy Week and Easter.

31

Mark 14:12–31
The upper room

We are now at Thursday, which Mark calls 'the first day of the festival of unleavened bread', because during the Passover season Jews eat only unleavened bread (as their ancestors did on that fateful night of their escape from Egypt). Jesus had obviously made quite detailed preparations for the Passover, including booking a room in Jerusalem for the Passover meal—the *Seder*, as it is called. It was a large upstairs room—the 'Upper Room' of Christian tradition.

As they began the meal, Jesus said that one of them would betray him. Judas was present and heard the warning of the consequences of that act, but, as we shall see, still went ahead with it.

During the Passover meal Jesus took the unleavened bread (the *matzos*), said the usual blessing, broke it in the traditional way to be shared by the company—but then added some startling new words of his own: 'This is my body'. We don't know what the disciples made of this drastic rewriting of the Passover ritual, but in any case more was to come. When Jesus took the cup of wine and said the blessing, he added, 'This is my blood which is poured out for many, my blood which seals God's covenant.'

The Passover was based on God's 'old' covenant with the people of Israel, an 'agreement' by which he was their God and they were his people. That covenant with Moses was sealed with the blood of a sacrificed lamb, and committed the people of Israel to obey God's commandments and so enjoy his blessing and protection.

Now, Jesus implied, a 'new covenant' had been negotiated—a covenant, or agreement, sealed with his own blood. His death would inaugurate this covenant, and under it those who believed in him would have forgiveness and become God's new people. So Jesus would be the new 'Moses', leading the people of God out of the era of slavery and death into the life of the kingdom of God.

Mark's account of the 'Last Supper', as it is called, is typically very brief! But the essentials are all there, even if we need to look at the other Gospel accounts, and the even earlier account in St Paul's first letter to the Corinthians (11:23–25), in order to get the full meaning of this event.

After the meal, Jesus's words of warning are rejected by Peter. Even if all the others were to abandon Jesus, he would stay loyal. The boast was an empty one. Jesus predicted that it wouldn't even last till morning!

32

Mark 14:32–52
Jesus is arrested

Jesus and his followers obviously used the garden of Gethsemane, on the Mount of Olives, as a place of prayer, well away from the noise and hubbub of the city. On this night—the night before his death—Jesus felt almost crushed by the horror of what lay ahead of him. His prayer in the garden should rule out any idea that because he was the Son of God the suffering he faced was somehow lessened. Jesus of Nazareth was truly human, and crucifixion was an appalling way of execution, involving prolonged and excruciating suffering.

His prayer investigates the possibility that the Father could find some other way—that 'this cup of suffering' might be taken away. Yet Jesus also knew his divine destiny. He was to be the 'suffering servant of God' prophesied by Isaiah. Only through the death of the Son of God could evil be finally defeated, and it was to defeat evil that he had come. So God's will was paramount: 'Not what I want, but what you want.' There is no better—or more difficult—prayer to pray than that.

While Jesus prayed in an agony, his disciples fell asleep! Their spirits might be willing, but their bodies were weak. He let them have some rest, only waking them when he became aware that the party of soldiers were making their way into the garden to arrest him.

The crowd who had come to arrest Jesus aren't given the dignity of the description 'soldiers' by Mark (though Luke calls them the 'temple guard' and John says the party consisted of both temple guards and Roman soldiers). But they were led by a figure identified by all the Gospels—Judas, 'one of the Twelve'.

When he greeted Jesus with the customary kiss, he made the phrase 'the kiss of Judas' into a synonym for the worst of all betrayals, the betrayal of a one-time friend. There was momentary resistance from one of the disciples (Peter, according to John's Gospel), but it was a futile gesture. They had come out for Jesus, as he said scornfully, as though he were an outlaw, having not dared to arrest him in public. He then added, 'But the Scriptures must come true'. His arrest was part of his God-given destiny.

At those words, all the disciples fled away into the darkness, including a 'certain young man', who eluded a grabbing hand which caught hold of his robe, and ran away naked. This little incident is recorded only in Mark's Gospel, and many experts think it can only refer to Mark himself, who would have been a young man in his late teens at this point. No wonder he remembered it!

33

Mark 14:53–72
Jesus stands alone

It was now deep into the night, but the high priest and his associates were in a hurry to get Jesus executed before the Passover sabbath, which began at nightfall on Friday. The formality of a 'trial' before the Council (the Sanhedrin), presided over by the high priest, was essential. Only the Roman governor, Pontius Pilate, could order an execution, but in an essentially religious case like this he would expect the Sanhedrin to present him with a convincing case against the accused. While Jesus faced the Council, Peter had plucked up enough courage to follow 'at a distance', and was now in the courtyard of the palace, warming himself by the fire.

The case against Jesus was very thin. He had threatened to destroy the temple single-handed, and rebuild it in three days. One can imagine what Pilate would have made of that story! And in any case the witnesses contradicted each other.

In the end, it was a straight question from the high priest which brought them what they wanted. 'Are you the Messiah,' he asked Jesus, 'the Son of the Blessed God?'

All through his ministry Jesus had avoided making any such claim himself. You will remember that he drew that confession out of the disciples, and probably others had arrived at that conclusion through hearing what he said and seeing what he did. But now the religious leader of Israel had asked him a straight question, and it got a straight answer: 'I am, and you will see the Son of Man seated on the right side of the Almighty...'

I dare say the Sanhedrin couldn't believe their luck! They had the evidence they needed. To claim to be the Messiah and the Son of God was manifestly blasphemous. Unless, of course, it was true...

They chose to believe that Jesus was a fraud, and their verdict was unanimous. He was guilty, and should be put to death. All that remained (though it was a big 'all') was to get Pilate's agreement to the execution.

Meanwhile, the career of Peter, extrovert leader of the Twelve, was about to hit rock bottom. Faced with questions from a servant girl, he swore an oath that he didn't even know Jesus. And at that moment the cock crowed. It was dawn, and another prophecy of Jesus had come true.

34

Mark 15:1–15

Before Pilate

Roman law is famous in history, and in many ways is the basis of much modern European law. The Romans were proud of their system of justice, and there is plenty of evidence that, at any rate by the standards of the ancient world, it was generally fair, if tough.

Pontius Pilate had been prefect, and then procurator (or governor) of the province of Judea since AD26. His rule had been marked by a number of violent clashes, mostly when he rode roughshod over Jewish religious scruples. He controlled the army, he alone had the right to enforce or revoke the death penalty, and—strangely, it seems—he controlled the temple and its funds, and even appointed the high priests.

Yet in the case of Jesus he seemed very hesitant... inclined to do what the crowd (and the temple leaders) wanted rather than what he plainly saw was right. In an attempt to avoid sending Jesus to the cross, he offered, according to an annual custom, to release a prisoner, expecting that the crowd would ask for Jesus. When they asked instead for Barrabas—a Jewish terrorist who had taken part in a violent uprising against the Romans—he seemed surprised. What then should he do with Jesus? 'Crucify him!' came the shout from the crowd.

The crowd was hardly a representative one, of course. After all, this was early morning, and the followers of Jesus were mostly in hiding. It seems probable that the priests had gathered together a mob of their own choosing. If they had, it worked. Pilate wanted no more trouble reported back to the emperor—there had been more than enough already. (In fact, he was summoned to Rome a few years later to answer charges of brutality, and was never heard of again.)

So he ordered Jesus to be whipped, and then handed him over to the soldiers to be crucified.

35

Mark 15:16–47
The crucifixion

Mark's account of the crucifixion is the most stark of all the Gospels. The death of Jesus is unrelieved by any human support (the women watched 'from a distance'). The passers-by mocked the dying man, inviting the one who had offered to save others to save himself. The dying thieves added their insults. And the whole scene was acted out in darkness, even though it was noonday—the darkness of eternal night, it must have seemed, and the victory of the powers of evil.

The awful cry of despair which came from the man on the cross emphasized the loneliness and isolation of his plight: 'My God, my God, why have you forsaken me?' It was in fact a quotation from a Psalm, a prayer to God for help in a time of desperate need. But did the help come?

As you read this scene, remind yourself who it was who was dying on the cross. This was no ordinary criminal, nor even a religious fanatic paying the price for extremism. This was the man whose hands had touched the sick, who gave sight to the blind, who opened deaf ears, who exercised power over darkness and evil in people's lives. This was the one who spoke and acted like the Son of God.

Now his awesome battle against evil had reached its climax, and he faced it alone. There was no human comfort or support in this account of his suffering, and even his Father seemed to have abandoned him. Darkness was the only appropriate backdrop, and darkness is what we have.

Not until Jesus was dead did the first shaft of light break, and that did not come from one of his friends, but from an army officer in charge of the execution. When he saw how Jesus died (and the wording is significant), he said, 'This man was really the Son of God.'

A Gentile and a worshipper of foreign gods, he couldn't have meant by that what either a Jew or a Christian disciple would have meant, but his testimony is all the more powerful for that. He must have seen many men die, but he had never seen one die like this.

There was at the same moment another sign of hope. The curtain in the temple divided the 'holy place', where it was believed that God was present in a special way, from the outer courts of the temple. Only the high priest could enter the holy place, on behalf of all the people— who were kept outside the curtain. The curtain stood for the barrier that keeps ordinary humans away from a holy God, but it also stood for the whole religious system of ancient Israel, based on a special priesthood and the offering of animal sacrifices.

At the moment Jesus died, Mark tells us, the curtain was torn in two—from top to bottom, notice, as though by some unseen heavenly hand. That symbolized the breaking down of barriers between God and the human race, and the end of the old order of priests and sacrifices for sin. Jesus, the Son of God, having confronted evil in his own body, had broken through on behalf of us all. The way to God was now open, and all could enter.

The male disciples had fled, except for Peter, who probably wished he had joined them. The women disciples, however, had followed Jesus all the way to Golgotha, the place of execution (it's called 'Calvary' in Latin). They had watched at a distance, it is true, but at least they were there, and now that Jesus was dead they were able to help with the last rites for the dead, the anointing and bandaging of the body. But it was now nearly evening, so the sabbath was near. Their last work of mercy would have to wait until Sunday morning. So they simply noted the cave-tomb—belonging to a member of the Council who was obviously a secret disciple of Jesus, Joseph of Arimathea—and watched as he sealed it with a large stone.

They would return on Sunday.

Mark 16:1–20
The resurrection of Jesus

Mark's sombre account of the crucifixion and death of Jesus ended, as we saw, with his body being simply wrapped in a burial sheet and placed in the tomb. Nothing could be done during the sabbath—the great day of the Passover, no less. But as soon as they could on Sunday morning some of the women who had faithfully followed Jesus (even when the male disciples deserted him) came to anoint his body.

They were aware of the problem of the heavy stone, but when they got to the place they discovered that it had already been rolled back. Not suspecting any supernatural explanation at this point, they went into the tomb.

That was when the real surprises started! The 'young man' whom they saw was clearly regarded by Mark as an angel, and his appearance filled them with utter awe and amazement—that's what is conveyed by the very unusual Greek word Mark uses.

The angel had a startling message. The crucified body of Jesus is 'not here' (that is, in the tomb) but alive. He has been 'raised' (as he had repeatedly told the disciples he would be). And they are to be the bearers of a message to the rest of the disciples that they would see him in Galilee.

It's very interesting that Peter is mentioned by name— and very generous! After all, the last we read of Peter he was denying that he even knew Jesus. Yet here he is invited by name to meet the risen Lord.

Not surprisingly, the women were emotionally overcome by this. Fear and awe in the face of so clearly supernatural an event are understandable. They fled from the tomb, but in their fear said nothing to anybody.

And that, believe it or not, is where Mark's Gospel actually ends! The remaining verses of this chapter, which give a summary of the various appearances of the risen Jesus to his disciples, were not part of the original manuscript. They are old—probably written early in the second century—and were recognized by the Church as part of the Christian scriptures, but they were not written by Mark. Why his Gospel ends so abruptly and (to the ordinary reader) leaving so many unanswered questions, is one of the great problems of New Testament scholarship—which we won't go into here!

What is obvious, though, is that even the 'cut-off' version gives all the essentials of the story of the resurrection of Jesus. That story, as Christians have received it, always has two basic elements: the empty tomb, and the appearances of the risen Jesus.

Mark is very clear about the empty tomb. You could say it is the main point that his story gets across. The women came to the tomb early, and found it empty. Not only that, but the angelic messenger was able to tell them why: not because the body had been moved or stolen, or because they'd gone to the wrong tomb, but because Jesus had been raised—exactly as he had consistently told them he would be.

Mark's truncated Gospel has no actual 'appearances' of Jesus to the disciples, but it does have a very specific promise that they would take place. The disciples would 'see him'. And the summary in verses 9–20 shows how that was fulfilled and how those appearances became part of the record of the early Church.

Mark has presented the story of Jesus as the confrontation between light and darkness, evil and absolute good. In the villages and lanes of Galilee Jesus faced and conquered the grim enemy, whether in the guise of physical sickness or handicap, or of inner turmoil and possession.

Finally, he faced the same enemy's last desperate stand, on the hill called Golgotha. There darkness did its worst, and the Son of Man bore it all and bowed his head in suffering and death. For a moment, it may have seemed as though evil had finally triumphed (though that torn temple curtain, and the words of the Roman soldier, gave us hints of what was to come).

Now, on the Sunday morning—what we call Easter day—the reality of the outcome was revealed. Evil did its worst, but Love has conquered. God has raised his Son from the dead. The grave is empty and the Saviour of the world is ready to meet his frightened followers and empower them to bear his message 'throughout the whole world'.

Love has the final word. In God's purposes it always does.

Angels

'Angels' occur at times throughout the Bible. They are spiritual beings seen as God's 'messengers' (which is the literal meaning of the Greek word used in the Gospels).

Their task is to convey God's messages to individuals, and to do it with his authority. Sometimes they appear to people in dreams (for example, to Joseph, in Matthew 1:20), but often there is a specific appearance to an individual (for example, to Mary the mother of Jesus, in Luke 1:26–27).

A message from an angel is equivalent to a message directly from God—that is the significance of the angel who appeared in the empty tomb.

If you have enjoyed reading *Mark for Starters*, you may wish to know that David Winter is a regular contributor to BRF's regular series of Bible reading notes, *New Daylight*, which is published three times a year (in January, May and September) and contains printed Bible passages, brief comments and prayers. *New Daylight* is also available in a large print version.

Copies of *New Daylight* may be obtained from your local Christian bookshop or by subscription direct from BRF.

A free sample copy of *New Daylight* containing two weeks of readings may be obtained by sending an A5 SAE marked '*New Daylight*' to BRF.

For more information about *New Daylight* and the full range of BRF publications, write to: The Bible Reading Fellowship, Peter's Way, Sandy Lane West, Oxford OX4 5HG (Tel. 01865 748227)